IT'S TIME TO EAT FRUIT SALAD

It's Time to Eat
FRUIT SALAD

Walter the Educator

Silent King Books
A WhichHead Entertainment Imprint

Copyright © 2024 by Walter the Educator

All rights reserved. No part of this book may be reproduced in any manner whatsoever without written per- mission except in the case of brief quotations embodied in critical articles and reviews.

First Printing, 2024

Disclaimer

This book is a literary work; the story is not about specific persons, locations, situations, and/or circumstances unless mentioned in a historical context. Any resemblance to real persons, locations, situations, and/or circumstances is coincidental. This book is for entertainment and informational purposes only. The author and publisher offer this information without warranties expressed or implied. No matter the grounds, neither the author nor the publisher will be accountable for any losses, injuries, or other damages caused by the reader's use of this book. The use of this book acknowledges an understanding and acceptance of this disclaimer.

It's Time to Eat FRUIT SALAD is a collectible early learning book by Walter the Educator suitable for all ages belonging to Walter the Educator's Time to Eat Book Series. Collect more books at WaltertheEducator.com

USE THE EXTRA SPACE TO TAKE NOTES AND DOCUMENT YOUR MEMORIES

FRUIT SALAD

It's time to eat, oh what a treat,

It's Time to Eat

Fruit Salad

A bowl of fruit that's fun to eat!

Colors so bright, red, green, and blue,

Delicious fruit, just for you!

The apples crunch, the bananas sweet,

Tiny blueberries can't be beat.

Oranges juicy, they drip and run,

Eating fruit is so much fun!

Grapes so round, like tiny balls,

Mango slices, the best of all.

Pineapple chunks with golden glow,

Into the bowl, watch it grow!

Strawberries red with little seeds,

Packed with vitamins, all we need.

Kiwi is fuzzy but oh so nice,

It's green and tangy, a perfect slice!

Mix it together, give it a toss,

Add a little honey, just a gloss.

A rainbow snack, so fresh and cool,

Fruit salad is the golden rule!

Crunch and chew, take a bite,

It's Time to Eat

Fruit Salad

Filling your tummy feels just right.

Healthy and yummy, it's so neat,

Fruit salad's the best to eat!

Sharing with friends is extra fun,

Pass the bowl to everyone!

Smiles and giggles fill the air,

Fruit salad shows we care.

Morning, noon, or in the night,

Fruit salad's always a delight.

A treat so sweet, a snack so grand,

Enjoy it with a spoon in hand.

One last bite, and then we say,

"Thank you, fruit, for a yummy day!"

Nature's gift, so fresh, so true,

Fruit salad is the best for you!

It's Time to Eat

Fruit Salad

Let's all shout, "Hooray, hooray!"

Fruit salad makes a brighter day.

Eat it up, feel strong and bright,

Fruit is power, pure delight!

ABOUT THE CREATOR

Walter the Educator is one of the pseudonyms for Walter Anderson. Formally educated in Chemistry, Business, and Education, he is an educator, an author, a diverse entrepreneur, and he is the son of a disabled war veteran. "Walter the Educator" shares his time between educating and creating. He holds interests and owns several creative projects that entertain, enlighten, enhance, and educate, hoping to inspire and motivate you. Follow, find new works, and stay up to date with Walter the Educator™

at WaltertheEducator.com

www.ingramcontent.com/pod-product-compliance
Lightning Source LLC
LaVergne TN
LVHW052012060526
838201LV00059B/3985